CW00531089

It was a wave
    that delivered us
        to this rock and a rock

    that placed us, shaken
but unbroken,
back upon that wave.

Between 2011 and 2014, poet and artist Gregory O'Brien found
himself following the migratory routes of whales and seabirds across
vast tracts of the South Pacific Ocean. O'Brien describes the poems
and drawings that resulted from these voyages, the work in this book,
as 'acts of devotion – a homage to a series of remarkable locations
and to the natural histories of those places'. An independent writer,
painter, literary critic and art curator, O'Brien has produced many
books of poetry, fiction, essays and commentary. Recent publications
with Auckland University Press include *Beauties of the Octagonal
Pool*, *A Micronaut in the Wide World* and the multi-award-winning
introductions to art *Welcome to the South Seas* and *Back and Beyond*.
A collection of poems written in Chile, *Citizen of Santiago*, with
photographs by Bruce Foster, was published by Trapeze in 2013.

WHALE YEARS
GREGORY O'BRIEN

AUCKLAND
UNIVERSITY
PRESS

For my fellow Kermadecians
and in praise of all Raoulies

First published 2015

Auckland University Press
University of Auckland
Private Bag 92019
Auckland 1142
New Zealand
www.press.auckland.ac.nz

ISBN 978 1 86940 832 9

Publication is kindly assisted by

A catalogue record for this book is available from the National Library of New Zealand

All images by Gregory O'Brien
Cover design by Spencer Levine

Cover painting: detail from *Lines composed a few miles above Our Lady of the
Antipodes, Pitt Island*, 2013; photograph by Dan du Bern, Tauranga Art Gallery.

Frontispiece: detail from *Raoul Island Whale Survey, with shipping containers,
Astrolabe Reef*, 2012; page 94: *Tuhua, Mayor Island, obscured by seabirds*, 2014;
both intaglio etchings printed at Michael Kempson's Cicada Press, Sydney.

Printed in China by 1010 Printing International Ltd

Contents

It is a genial region, with a delightful climate
and exempt from every harmful blast . . .
all discord and sorrow is unknown.
– PLINY

Ask me to describe this whole beautiful thing
Well, if I were a bell, I'd go ding dong, ding dong ding.
– 'IF I WERE A BELL', FRANK LOESSER, 1950

If you can tilt the field then you will dislodge certain objects in the
field and your own prepossessions may be dislodged as well.
– WILSON HARRIS

He had bought a large map representing the sea,
Without the least vestige of land:
And the crew were much pleased when they found it to be
A map they could all understand.
– LEWIS CARROLL, FROM 'THE HUNTING OF THE SNARK'

'It's not air that you look for in a painting, it's the bottom of the
ocean.'
– YANCO VARDA, IN AGNÈS VARDA'S FILM *ONCLE YANCO*

All personnel will need to be able to ascend and descend ladders with
ease, and need to be able to grip, reach, pull, push, squat, lift, carry,
climb and jump in order to participate safely.
– NAVAL INSTRUCTIONS FOR SEARIDERS, HMNZS *OTAGO*

Don't let the herring swim over your head.
– FLEMISH PROVERB

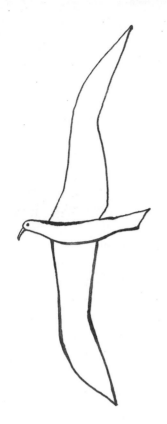

ONE   FROM VARIOUS ISLANDS

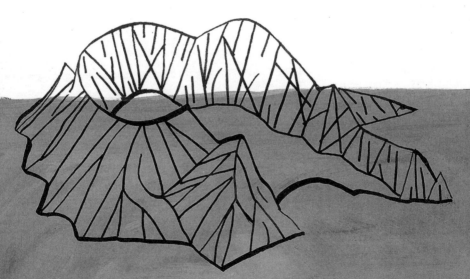

The length of the voyage

As measured by buckets of salt water

As measured by the shadow of a pohutukawa, variations thereof

As measured by the pollen remaining in the seams of a jacket

As measured by the number of flying fish landed on the deck

As measured by the names of seamounts laid in an unstraight line

As measured by everything in the rope room that is not rope

As was once measured by crayfish

As measured by rocks brought from a far island, a sign of respect

As measured by every previous voyage and every subsequent voyage
from now
     until the end of time.

Raoul Island

By frigate and bird
we came ashore

fresh-footed on the swaying
headland, by balloon boat

and a piece of
yellow twine. Here we were

set down, buffered in
moss and lichen, riding

the undulations of the seaward lawn – and this
was our unrest. We walked

the edible path, an orchard of oranges
underfoot, mushrooms

like satellite dishes tilted
at the sky. We followed

the flight paths of petrel and red-tailed
tropic bird, of grey ternlet

and masked booby – and theirs was
the song the island sang.

Emotional life of Thomas Bell, Raoul Island

The lake in the poem
depends upon
who stands

before it – Hettie or Bess
or, most likely,
Mary.

It might have been
the Blue or
the Green –

or maybe lakes
had no names
back then?

The hills moved
instinctively
north

or, less often, south
and the transient
Wolverine Rock

which kept reappearing
offshore, but only
upon the birth

of a daughter, was neither
here nor there.
The weather takes

the edges off most things.
The island tethered
or set adrift

depending on which
daughter dives
into which

lake. But it is their eyes
I remember most
not as they

looked, but as they
looked
at me

or at someone who stood
where I stand
as if to lose

what I have lost.

Whale Survey, Raoul Island, with Rosemary Dobson

Two poets on a headland, mid-survey
might pause suddenly and say
will this be your whale, or mine?

Moving, accordingly, from one observation area
to the next, a whale is 'handed over'.
Please take it. No, you first.

Early morning spent 'getting the eye in'
velocity of clouds, sea conditions noted.
Breaching, logging, travelling, the Pacific

divided between Coral Bay and Tropic Bird Face,
Bomb Shed, Hutchies Bluff and Blindspot. Later
Rosemary observed to a friend

from the sharpest point of her triangulation:
If I stand still enough, I can see Wolverine Rock,
a water spout and, westerly, one cow and calf.

The captain of the Rena on Astrolabe Reef

He might have been sharpening up on the sea, as the sea was
sharpening its points. A Number Two, he was told.
The crew was looking sharp, to a point.

From point to point of a chart – and all points north of
the Point of Saying Goodbye. A man goes out on a rib – a point
of departure. A point upon which

they disagreed or agreed to differ. A spike in the weather
another barbed or pointed front approaching. This time
a Number Four Sea. There were other points

of interest, distraction or contention. A compass or protractor
with its pointed readiness, a line following
the point of a pencil from this to that

point. Not to put too fine a point on the matter, the point being
a pointed hull run aground on a pointed reef,
if you get my drift, what is the point in that?

Oneraki

With beaches I am often
in agreement

       their slow
shuffle, organisational
skills

       oblivious to
whatever traffic
or freight is consigned

them. A beach is never
anybody's opinion

       of a beach –
as much wave
as sandy gradient

       where the ocean
leaves its coloured pencils, left-
footed jandals . . .
       Like a beach, I take

what I am given. As
a believer, I too am inhabited by
a fish
       or as a wave is
laid gently to
one side – such is
       the character of waves, the way
they are
       always hurrying

back
to themselves.

White Island (Whakaari)

Her highness and
lowness, her whiteness
and wilderness

untrammelled and
well-travelled, sister
ship, satiated

and sailed upon,
whiteness of her eyes
a pale flock, her
        gullness.

A schematic analysis of the first and only book of the explorer Raoul H. Rangitahua (page numbers in brackets)

In the ocean, he encounters a rock that can speak (15), a plume of smoke that could be a cloud (or, surely, a cloud that might be a plume of smoke?) and an assortment of volcanic stones on a headland, scattered or thrown randomly (24). He meets a nymph (25), who leads him through a grove of uprooted trees (27). In the ruins of what appears to be an ancient civilisation, he encounters green parrots (31) and a great many seabirds nested beneath the ground upon which he walks (33). He watches a balloon go up and feels he is observing the passing of a world (38). Because there is no livestock on the island, the shepherds oversee empty fields (41); some inadvertently become experts at the identification of sea turtles or whales in the far distance (42). He is ceremoniously joined to his new home through encounters with the last rat on the island, a mechanical replica, kept as a cautionary presence (43); two iron bed-frames left on a clifftop, possibly to memorialise the tragedy of two lovers (44); a dog kennel with the name 'Tui' above the entrance (45). To his dismay, he realises that the mules he was expecting to transport him, and his not inconsiderable luggage, around the rim of the volcano are, in fact, vehicles with four wheels and internal combustion engines (46). He heads off into the bush to regain some equilibrium (49) and encounters a crater containing a green lake and a blue lake (49). Everywhere he walks, he encounters graves (62). A well-mown lawn memorialises a cherished precursor (66). He ponders the sacrifices and triumphs of earlier inhabitants (67). With his companions, he struggles to erect a tent – a reprise of an engagement, on an earlier voyage, with a giant, mythological bird (80). After a crisis, he finds solace in the sunrise, a redness he likens to the complexion of an embarrassed deity (86). He is eventually led by a nymph back down to the edge of a strong, running sea (139). On Cupid's boat he is taken out beyond the breakers (142). The singing nymphs can be heard above the crashing waves (143). The winged boat is particularly at home amidst the flying fishes. His narrative ends with a grey vessel on a grey sea (148). He is enfolded in sleep (151), the dream preceding the sleep, the sleep preceding the dream.

A summer of inflatable gifts, Pitt Island

Gone the way of all air-
filled things, the first whale
never reached the water, was left

a moment too long on the
compressor. Wary, our children
accompanied the remaining pod

to Flower Pot Bay. Later, head-high
in scurvy grass, a game of hide-
and-seek claimed them, the untended

flotilla disappearing south. Also among
the departures, a sea-horse, butterfly and
coiled serpent. Evening, it dawned

on the teary young, their
knee-deep valediction, while
at the southern end of Flower Pot-

Glory Road, the black sand went about
its daily work, releasing the bones
of Moriori, centuries buried,

trussed and seated, as was custom,
facing the ocean. Each skull
an amphitheatre or occasional vase

of spear-grass and sow thistle, eased
seawards now by wind and hoof.
Westerly swell of nocturnal

sand, torchlight of human bones, and
this last outcrop the vanished whales
go around, the red admirals.

Weather balloon, Raoul Island

We sent him up, never to come
back down:
       the god of this island
is a hot air balloon

pale, inscrutable, rising above
green lake and cloud forest.

We let him go
       on the seaward lawn
trailing his coral-white laboratory
from whence

to transmit back to us
       immensities, unimaginable
altitudes, the intelligence

of ages. Mid-morning, the god
of each new day
       is raised
like bread on a baker's table
and set adrift

continuing upwards until
his ever-increasing god-head
       explodes and he rejoins

the older gods – frigate bird,
reef shark and flying fish –

in the aloneness
of the crowded sea.

13

Loneliness of the Raoul Island weather balloon

weather balloon

whether balloon

whenever balloon

whether we goest and from
    whence we come balloon

whither balloon

with-her balloon

      without-her balloon

wither balloon

The return of Christ to Futuna Chapel

The combined height of three plain-clothed
policemen, or the length, unfurled, of an orange
shawl – how else to measure

the returning bird-man, the weight of him
free-standing or afloat, lifted
from a white unmarked van.

Flesh of the wooden sea-swallow, sap
of his veins, unwound from a rain-drenched blanket
and restored in grey wall-space, partitioned light.

So it must be, in good time, the tree god is
reclaimed by the ordinary forest, the storm
petrel returned to the storm.

Whale years

for Phil Dadson

South-west Pacific

Ocean-sound, what is it
you listen for?

L'Esperance

Anchorstone, sea urchin
waterlogged instrument, tunes
a shrimp whistles.

Rekohu/Chatham Island

If there is
a moon
it is carved into
a dark tree. If
there is
a tree. But
there is always
an ocean.

Orange supply, Raoul Island

Bird rattle of
a cyclone-tossed greenness
ever-decreasing orchard.

Tongatapu

Your eyes were canoes, your brows
outriggers, your hair a wind-tossed
palm, and your bones
an ocean-polished whiteness.

Orongo, Rapa Nui

Easy on the oar
Steady the sail
Hold the thought
Let go the hand

Easter Fracture Zone

In the book of the ocean each wave
is recorded, but the lives of men are left
where they lie.

Plumeria rubra, Tongatapu

    aFter
    spRing
    cAme
    aN
   anGular
  musIc
     Piano
      Accordianist
    fiNgering
everythIng

Quintay, Chile

Everything I heard or
did not hear: the ocean
peeled back, wave by
wave, sigh of a once
whale-laden ocean.

Tongatapu

An ocean never dropped
a fish. The day's first lesson –
'A Quality Education for Now
& Eternity' – at the Ocean of Light
      School, Nuku'alofa.

~

Just beyond a billboard advertising
Rising Sun Beer
uncertainly, dawn flickers.

Hanga Roa, Rapa Nui

It is written. The chickens
of this island
laid only blue and green
eggs. It is written
a large wave came for them.
It is written.

Kermadec

Vast continent of
every tilted or rolling
thing – eyes and teeth
of implausible fish, stars
and planets on their
undersea orbits.

Southern Pacific Ocean

Arms and legs of
the plundered sea, for whom is it
you dance?

Rekohu

HIGH   SEA   LOW

LAND   LOW   SEA

HIGH   LAND   LOW

Raoul

Ghost shark, anvil,
kite

starboard, wind-
ward, my childhood

on Raoul Island
sustain me.

Pest eradication programme, Tuhua

With the last rats and mice
and the drinkers offloaded
        at South East Bay
the Cruising Club buried, conveniently,
in a landslip –
        all we now count on:
the numbered days of the numberless
        wasps of Mayor Island.

In advance of an oil slick, Bay of Plenty

Light and colour are
we are told
collisions. How then
in the absence of both,
mid-night, mid-ocean
the MV Rena on course
for Astrolabe Reef?

21

Oneraki Beach, Raoul Island

Unbreaking rocks
Broken sea

Unbroken sea
Breaking rocks

Waiheke Island Water Supply

On lancewood and five finger
twiggy coprosma
        and lemonwood, rain

and the memory of
rain and the persistence
    of all that is not rain

but upon which
    rain falls.

Sunrise, Mayor Island

Obsidian fish
glittering
in its red bucket.

Isla Negra, Chile

Telescope tree
what do you see?
Hummingbird
what have you heard?

Obsidian Headland, South East Bay

When the tin hull strikes
the glass headland
      the island rings
like a bell. And the boat, also
perfectly pitched.

Westerly over Te Whanga Lagoon, Rekohu

Great tongue, speak
now or forever
enfold us

in ribbonwood and matapo

indigenous flower
forget me not
forsake me now.

Off Mayor Island

A school of kahawai
the educated eye's
encyclopediae.

Kermadec Trench

Were there words
to inscribe
in this blueness

lines for the placation
of a storm god
delirious mathematics

of the deep, every
living thing with which
the ocean is awash.

Quintay, Chile

Mariners can read the ocean
as you would a book, each wave
the upturned corner of a page.

Pitch

In the fallen nikau forest, a tui
in two halves, two halves
of a song, sung.

Tuhua

wave-sharpened
headland, headland-
sharpened wave

Te Whanga Lagoon

STILL	ECHOING
ECHOING	STILL
STILL	ECHOING
ECHOING	STILL
STILL	ECHOING
ECHOING	STILL
STILL	ECHOING
ECHOING	STILL
STILL	ECHOING
ECHOING	STILL
STILL	ECHOING
ECHOING	STILL

Star of Bengal Bank

Everything overheard
or lost from
hearing: song of

coral palm and
one-eyed urchin, chapter
and verse of

the Isaiah-fish, bird-
burrowed sea
in which we dive down

and are retrieved. That
which light enters so
as never to leave.

Oneraki Beach, Raoul Island

I was raised by rocks, but not
as one of them. Upended
by storms, I was raised
by nikau palms, but I was never
one of them. I was raised by waves –
the waves talking, always talking
to themselves, always listening –
and raised as one of them.

South-east Pacific

Ocean-sound, what is it
you listen for?

A burning tyre, Nuku'alofa

With guavas and Pablo Neruda, we came
to the greenness

of this land, but our attempts
to meet the king

came to nothing. Confined to the blackness
of my shell, I was a crab

tied in red string, well-positioned
at the royal feast, but not

as I would have wished.
That I might speak

briefly with his highness
of such things

as weigh upon me. To the foreshore
I fled, while in the distance

his crab-shaped crown shook
its pincers at the sun.

Unfathomable morning,
these things heavy

upon my heart, I sought counsel
amidst the graves

of his ancestors – four corners of the sky
held in place

by volcanic boulders – and beneath
the unmoving clock faces

of his kingdom. Minute hands, hour hands . . .
I waved my pincers

in bafflement. Together, you and I
sought instead

the company of shellfish – those lowliest
citizens of this island –

in the mudflats where immigrant families
competed with pigs

for mussels. Later, you were a weather balloon
that you might gain

his attention, but as the day wore on
you were caught in an updraft

above the Cathedral of
the Burning Tyre – and it was not a done thing

to be higher than
his kingliness.

Nightfall, we were both
brass instruments

of the Royal Army Band – that we might
phrase our questions

in a language he understood. But,
for the sound of ourselves,

we could not hear
a word of his reply. Not for

the sirens of a sinking ferry, brakes
and stammering exhaust of the royal carriage –

a London cab crossing
the potholed kingdom.

Luminosity

*Bioluminescence is the ability of organisms to create
and emit light . . . it exists in 90 per cent of the animals
living in the open ocean, in waters below 500 metres . . .*
– SMITHSONIAN NATIONAL MUSEUM OF NATURAL HISTORY

When we met we were
          nothing if not
                    luminous. I remember it. Disarming
          you were
but seldom debilitating.
          Your state of undress rarely
                    accidental. Certain countries
          and climes were more
amenable – something
          to do with bathing
                    as distinct from
          swimming. Beach access
was desirable
          but never
                    indispensable. At times
          the captain's hat
would go, like a bird
          from head to head
                    only to increase the luminosity
          of all concerned – the beholder
and the beheld.
          But what is a little
                    luminosity among friends
          or in polite company?
I was reduced
          by it yet, unnecessarily
                    some would say,
          enhanced. In deference
to the classical tradition

and an encroaching Romanticism
                you would hurry down
        the corridor
outside the life room.
                Students of Life, all of us
                        or so we dreamed.
                But what did we know?
Only a fraction of
                what there was. Entire
                        caravans and beach houses
                had been devoted to the study
of you; libraries had groaned with
                the weight or velveteen
                        lightness of your literature.
                This little I was
certain of: 4am, you were wearing
                nothing but
                        the beam of a passing car
                a moment's torch-light
or the half
                of it – an intermittent gleam
                        reminding us that
                63 per cent of the human body
is water (or
                to put it another
                        way, 63 per cent
                of nakedness is
ocean). Eventually
                the body forgets
                        or is forgotten about.
                Adrift upon
the wide sea of
                itself. Other times you were
                        an aquarium
                a wet-land or
weather-station –
                I have this from

reliable sources –
a distant colony
of yourself.
Or you resembled
the voyage itself
with its exclamations
'Don't lean out too far'
or 'I think this must be
the island.'
You were present
but not accountable
as something seen
through a telescope
a starless night – less than
the calcium in your bones
or a sideways glance
across a room
late summer
a blanket that flooded
the house, your dress –
if it was a dress –
gathered and folded
and laid to one side.
It's not that I needed this
or need it now:
Luminosity, it might be upon us
you are bestowed
but you are never confined
by us. In this world
of unimaginable scarves and
tights, we seek you out.
Ill-planned, at other times
sadly mistaken. On your account
I have dipped my head above
and below water-line,
unencumbered yet
chaste. I never wanted for
directions. You were my skilled

and unskilled labour, the one
              to which, in a more congenial breeze
                    leaves might affix themselves
              in this, the garden
of cultivated acquaintance
              and which, only now, in the fading
                    the constantly fading light
              I have difficulty remembering.
Remind me.

What are heavy? sea-sand and sorrow:
What are brief? today and tomorrow:
What are frail? spring blossoms and youth:
What are deep? the ocean and truth.
– CHRISTINA ROSSETTI

O my lord, what shall I do with all this great material?
When shall these thousand planks be a work of art . . . ?

– MIDDLE IRISH EPIGRAM

TWO   BOOK OF NUMBERED DAYS

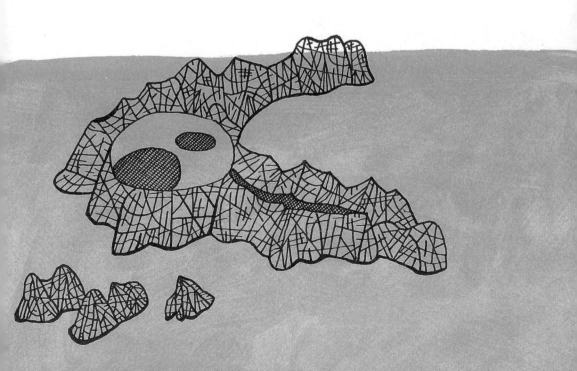

I South-west Pacific: Nuku'alofa, Tonga, May 2012

Longitudinal

Lie down Month of May
then stand up
and be gone. Or stay

and sing to us
but not so we
remember

the words, but so
this evening
remains intact

the almost-frozen
papaya, aftertaste of
chilled banana, a greenness

toppling into darkness
then back into
greenness, at the centre of which

a man is a way station
a stepping stone,
his thoughts always

half way
between one thing
and another

as
an island
is.

A crown for the new King of Tonga

Firstly, as ordained, the grassy expanse is cut by hand, with a thousand well-honed knives. Thereupon the Royal Undertakers are convened and the royal grave is dug, also by hand, using small fragments of coconut shell. Five hundred kilometres of purple and black drapery is flown from China, and the entire country embarks upon one hundred days of mourning. Around the island, countless objects are wrapped in purple and black: roadside signs, buildings, a goat, a coffee plantation. For the hundred days and nights of mourning, the fourteen undertakers are confined to the gravesite, sheltering beneath a purple and black tarpaulin which, from time to time, billows upwards in the onshore breeze – an airy crown for this, the newest King of Tonga, Death.

Hemisphere

Gramophone lizard
funnel head or dog-collar

lesser member
of the royal household

long may you linger
above the seasonal balcony

where our afternoons are spent
cracking open coconuts,

the long horizon
of the machete slicing

each coconut-sun –
a Tropic of Capricorn

from which milk
flows.

A common grave, Tongatapu

Items on a shelf. Pumice
mostly, and in
        an adjacent cemetery

a quilt or
blanket raised
        or laid upon

a mound – bottle blue
and frangipani
        freshly squeezed

cerulean. It is death
brightens this dark day –
        the recently departed

high above
the wide lagoon
        of our loss

of them, birds encircling
as we ourselves are
        planetary, orbiting

        this star-laden mound.

Nocturne

Stand up, Month of
July or
      August, your earthly body

forever drifting
back to us, stretching as far as
      Big Mama Yacht Club

where the seasonal voyagers
hove to – Hoki Mai, Wet Nose,
      then later

My Girl Pipistrelle. It comes
to this: the names
      of cruising vessels

learnt by heart – Lullaby, Lady
Nada, Night Cap,
      Windpony and Sputnik,

Cries and Whispers, Runaway Bunny,
Monkeyfeet,
      Slip Away – and the migratory

whales of Vavau navigating
by star and pillow
      past us, the undreamt whales

idling shorewards as
my sleeping head to
      your wide-awake body.

Two trees

One tree is wretched
for the health

of its fruit, another
has many hands

juggling, in the half-light
the ripening spheres.

Coconut crab, lizard and a bus called 'Psalm 23'

Palm thief or robber crab, there are
other names we have for you
as you would have

for us. Tupou College Mascot,
Well Travelled Egg, your pincers
remove a finger as easily

as they cut a fine horizon
around a coconut husk
before you climb inside. You are a reminder

of this kingdom's great virtues: a tenacious hold
on particulars, a propensity for
tree climbing and

against all odds, for reaching a good age –
your sixty crab-years
just under the human average. Also a common

ingenuity, lately applied to mourning:
a purple and blackness draped over
every freestanding thing: a basket

of coconuts, satellite dish, the street-front
of *Sandy Boyz Motel*. Even the underwater
mangrove roots of Pangaimotu Island

enshrouded in purple ribbon, visible
only at low, low tide –
that mourning time.

Elsewhere, a guitar amplifier and
the encumbered palm across which
the loudspeaker lizard

makes his way – there are names
we have for him too, as we have
for the Halaleva bus, 'Psalm 23'

intoned affectionately,
as we all go
       down this rough road.

Mourners of the death of the King of Tonga

What is the month of May
to a dead king

      and what is it
to those left behind?
We come to this

      'low, huddled shore'
following the migratory routes
of stones
      from outer islands –

the further these funereal rocks
have travelled the greater
      respect paid. The lesson

of the lop-sided canoe
the itinerant granite:
      what lies beneath us
will one day lie above us. It is written

the dead belong only
to the living, having
      left themselves

far behind. It is the mourners
the rock-carriers
      to whom we pay

our respects, mid-morning
my heart goes out
single-hulled, well-paddled
      to them.

Handbook for the recovery of sea turtles

Conveniently, they sleep on the seabed. A skilful diver might
descend a good ten metres and uplift one without waking it.
But it is even more effective to take a firm hold, one hand on
either side of the shell, and give the creature a shake. Startled,
it will instinctively make for the surface. You hold on for the
ride. With a boat and net nearby, it is relatively easy, from there,
to remove the sea turtle from the sea.

If you manage to spear one flipper, that flipper will retract
and the turtle will start swimming in circles. You can continue
hunting elsewhere and, when you return, the turtle will
still be there, orbiting the exact point where you speared it,
spiralling up to the surface to breathe, then spiralling hopelessly
downwards again.

There are bad times of year, but undoubtedly the worst time
to be a turtle in coastal waters is shortly after the death – or,
alternatively, before the coronation – of a king. The feasting on
such occasions requires upward of three hundred mature turtles.

Tapa

Lie down, Month of May
and June
      and July, your noble subjects
hauled from or returned, like
seabed turtles, to
sleep –

the cat that lives inside
   the dog, the out-of-luck bird
the esteemed chickens of Rapa Nui in
their rocky citadels, overseeing
      the lesser affairs of men –

such tales they tell us
of over-arching horizon
      and quarried sea. And all of this
is recorded in
      the tapa, and all of this
is spoken to me
by the paperbark cloth.

A liberal economy

So broadcasts the loudspeaker
lizard, a hymn

in praise of the Royal Tongan
Satellite Programme,

the law-abiding tuna fleets of fair, distant
lands, fishing rights

for local fishers, mobile telephones for
banana palms.

Lamp and lizard

Motionless, you move
us, Lizard. In your studious light
we read ourselves
        to sleep. High Commissioner,
your neck-dress
is frilled, Elizabethan,
        a precisely calibrated loudspeaker
for the silent, queenly voice

a funnel-neck in which
moths as well as words
        are corralled.
Shuttlecock, beacon –
if silence were a radio station

then you would be
        a broadcaster, the searchlight beam
of your head gone far
into a night-sky
        where satellites are retrieved
by your long tongue, and the long body
it attends . . . Reading lamp, by which
I observe the Evening Office
        the Riot Act, the last words
of King George Tupou V, you render
this mumbling world
        articulate, as a book
well-written then well-read
        under your flickering light.

A hundred days of mourning

Lie down, Month of June, and then
pretend to go,
            a hundred days gone
the kingdom, unwrapped, hardly recognises
            itself. Parliament resumes;
the palm thief finds
            a new shell – Tafi beer can or
plastic jug – and the streets are ablaze
with brass bands and school uniforms.
Every moving
                        or immovable thing
filled to the brim

as the earth is now filled. And that also
            is a part
                        of mourning,
            as well as, almost, an end
to it.

II *South-east Pacific: Rapa Nui/Easter Island, July 2012*

Del Pacifico Sudeste

Tangler of twine and fishing wire, we
have woken more than once
to the sound of you – salt-eyed, krill-enriched
      turtle-hungry – we have launched

our boats across your scarred
back, thrown our quivering lines
beyond your curved horizon.

It is emptiness that fills
this earth

      hollowness this sky, but
when I think of you, first
I think of Neruda's swaying captains

on their swaying hill. Following sea, running
      sea, great sea of the unmade mind
you are always between
islands, like this song, entangled
in your own lines –

      one part water, two parts
            sky – my distant head
your unfathomable body.

At Tongariki

We reach out
and touch

what is forever

and what is
forever

beyond reach.

Gravestone

The same gulls wheeling above the cemetery
at Hanga Roa
       trawling for

the names of the dead. Each cry
a half-remembered inscription
lifted high above the headland.

Tangerine

Amelia sends me a star chart. No,
I am mistaken, it is a map of underwater volcanoes –
a handbook of invisible seamounts

above which the heart
sends out its research vessels
to gather samples and specimens, to record

places of departure and arrival, this
interminable shaking. My botanist friend, she
questions my deliberations.

The banana, she tells me, is hardly a plant
let alone a tree. Like ginger
it is a perennial herb.

I devote the rest of the day to
eating mandarins, at least
I think they are mandarins.

South-east Pacific

A hurried sky, quickening sea, a voice

Curved planks of the sea turtle, a voice

The cemetery dogs, a voice

A fishing boat called M. Jesus Joe, a voice

A baked chicken plucked from a lawn, a voice

And another voice, always another voice
      in reply.

On Easter Island

The great voyages of Polynesian history, of Cook
and Lapérouse and Thor Heyerdahl's Kon-Tiki
      as nothing compared

to the everyday transit, by Southern Pacific Gyre
of one bucket, a left-footed jandal and two plastic containers
marked 'Property of Sanfords, South Island, New Zealand'.

Apparition of the head of a Chilean dictator as a moai, Easter Island

Bonegrinder, toothpuller
president of all
our sleepless nights
the eyeless moai of Rapa Nui

stare down the prison-blocks
of the years, your horse-drawn casket
still churning dust, a mound
of steaming manure overshadowing

La Moneda. From this far province,
we wish you a bad night's sleep,
Generalissimo, may our
volcanic unrest forever rattle

your antique limbs and arthritic heart, may you be
dissembled, chicken-pecked, horse-
trodden, never to be made whole again
in this or any other universe.

Elegy

The disappeared
are always

with us, it is emptiness
fills the earth.

Luck Bird

My feast day an occasion of some solemnity.
It arrives, as any other, by sea – my nesting place
and vantage point, from where I behold
this world's wonders – a black cat

eating a cucumber, the magnetic navel
of a woman, a boy with dog meat
between his teeth – and the song
allocated each of them, the accompanying guitar

made from the shell of a crab or turtle
or armadillo. And, mindful of
the implications of this, on the far mainland,
ever cautious, a crab, a turtle and an armadillo.

Hanga Roa

The first night awoke
to a lizard crowing

like a rooster, a card game
that sounded

like rain on a tin roof . . .
a dog had fallen

from a tree, a house was
built upon a horse.

Guitar, Hanga Roa

Eight-stringed and night-long
strummed, you prove yourself

a necessary accompaniment on these
longest of evenings. Bigger

than a fish-scale, smaller than the sky
how do your songs describe you?

Wider than a sardine, narrower
than the sea. Sing to us

of how, in this world of untimely things,
a man might also be defined –

half way between a grass skirt
and a headstone, a mollusc

and an ocean liner. Mid-way between
a hammer and a wind-tossed

palm. No, upon reflection
do not tell us, Guitar. Sing instead

only of your strings and not
of how this world is strung.

Headstone lamps, Hanga Roa

Midnight's luminescence, hilltop graveyard
speckled with solar-powered bulbs
          glowing jellyfish, beacons
for the renavigation of
moonlit depths. Here on the sea floor
of the slender-fingered ones
          we swim upwards
the deep sea creatures we once were
we are again.

Conversation between a stone head on Easter Island and the weather balloon, Raoul Island

1.

Stone head, cliff face
you would have us
bury our noses in
rich volcanic soil or vanish

beneath a whale-trammelled
sea. Wedged between one world
and the next, you measure time
as we are measured

by it. Grand-
father clock, waist-deep
in the quarry of the self, you are
both a man's idea of a stone

and a stone's idea
of a man, your unfathomable
body swallowed whole
by your distant, proximate head.

2.

Wind-bag, balloon-brain
each morning miraculously
reborn, adrift
in the updrafts, convections,

we tether our words
to you, that we might be free
of them, that they might
plummet, mid-ocean, into

the impossibility of our retrieving
you. In return, we praise your
aptitude, Icarus-bird, maestro of the moment,
scale model of this finite planet

pale, woebegone, you are expelled
from this incomparable blueness, summarised,
made smaller, enfolded inside
        your falling.

Moai, Rapa Nui

This is our place.
You can't touch mourning

it is mourning
          touches you.

It's gone. It's here. The life
everlasting, the life

that suddenly
never was.

The non-disappeared, Hanga Roa

Monthly, the gravestones
are replenished, overwritten
      in felt pen or chalk

the occasional daub
of white paint; at times
a name will change
      or be revised, contested. No matter

we are all in this
together – on this seaward incline
      overlooking

the afterlife. But all we can see
from here
      lights of incoming
          fishing boats.

The zoo above our heads

When the creaking, bird-heavy clouds
above Anakena shuffle
        their electrical selves, the nerves

be frayed. I follow the flittering neurons
as far back
as Santiago Zoo
        on its hilltop perch, its low-flying
population of chimpanzees with names
like Nixon and Kissinger
        and the monkey with
the shiniest buttons, Milton Friedman. Some evenings
        it is as if the contents
      of the Santiago Zoo have
fallen upon our heads. Yet, here on Rapa Nui, how mightily
        the mighty have already fallen
that ruinous
brigade of gods and ancestors
        the deflated balloon-man Pinochet
and King George Tupou V, all of them

face-down, upended
and presiding over all:
        the blue and green eggs, the aerial
chicken coops of Rapa Nui
and the turtle-sun rattling the cages.

At Orongo

My stone
head

your earthly
body

our ocean.

A children's song, Hanga Roa

Fishing Boat, Little Fish
the swell is always taller
than you, the waves

more numerous. Thrown around
in any weather, you drink
far too much. Fishing Boat

Little Fish, you trawl your own
shadow. It is the plenitude of fishes
that keeps you afloat,

the constellations and electrical
gravestones of Hanga Roa that guide you
home. Fishing Boat

Little Fish, your family
above, your family
below – creature of air

and water, the oceans of the world
are yours to ply, but today
your only catch will be
       this song.

The sky above Rapa Nui

Salt grinder of stars
pepper grinder of night
what is it you listen for?

Groan of a straining
oarsman, mispronunciation
of the Spanish language

by the waves at Anakena
my wide-awake head
your sleeping body?

Church at Hanga Roa

And so, Easter Island, I go out, but not so far
as to lose sight of you; I go out

not so far as to
dream. And I dream
  not so as to leave your body

but to remain there
as one might
  a sloping field.

The well-angled stone skims across
water
  but labours on land

as does man, that
hollow egg or sinking ship
  palm-brained, run aground

yet somehow
always with us
  and in us. Remember

the Luck Bird, installed
crown-like on the Virgin's head –
  unholy, yet somehow

blessed. We are all
such fortunate souls
  such eggs the Luck Bird

  lays for us.

Somewhere our belonging particles
Believe in us. If we could only find them.
– W. S. GRAHAM, 'IMPLEMENTS IN THEIR PLACES'

This earth that bears you up is a handful of sand [yet] it holds
The Flower Mount and Dog Mountain without feeling the
weight of them; Hoang Ho, the river, and the oceans surge
and the earth loses not a drop of their waters, holding them in
their beds, containing the multitude of their creatures.
– CONFUCIUS/EZRA POUND

It is the aim of every ship-master to prevent his vessel running
aground or coming into uncontrolled contact with jetties and
quays or with other vessels.
– THE DUMPY BOOK OF SHIPS & THE SEA

The stones roll out to shelter in the sea.
– W. S. GRAHAM, SHIAN BAY

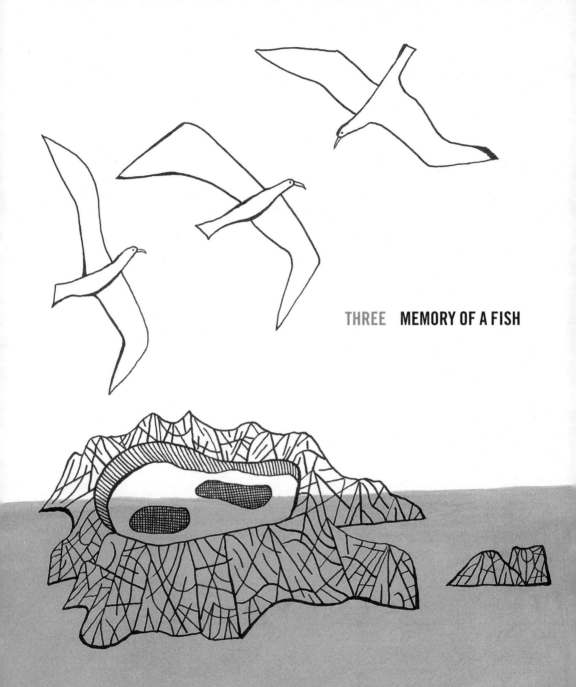

THREE **MEMORY OF A FISH**

For Felix,
recently returned from
the Kermadec Islands

An albatross never flew
in a poem by Charles Baudelaire
    nor gulped saltwater and fish

        and the nation of Chile
    never dipped its beak
into the Pacific

but for a tray
    of ginger slice
        and the steaming, volcanic teapot

    we shared, mid-ocean,
on this north-facing slope
while birds grazed

        the fruit-laden lawn
            and a tui hopped
    blindly towards us

its head stuck
inside a grapefruit.
    I imagined you

        long-spined, musically
    inclined, breathing into
your melodica –

mournful phrases
    cut adrift, far
        from home

        counting each note
    just as, last October
south by Raoul Island,

126 whales accounted for
    a single morning of the annual survey.
        The same way we followed

    the northerly migration of
shipping containers from the MV Rena
wrecked that same month

    on Astrolabe Reef.
        Hours before the collision,
Noel had phoned

from Napier, watching
the vessel leave harbour
    with its swaying

        container-towers and
    erratic navigation. It was as if,
he observed, the children

had driven off
    with the family car. But no one
        said a word

    as it steamed out
of the deregulated harbour
sailing forth into

    deregulated night
        navigating by a sky of
hapless constellations. Or was it

the shades of politicians past –
ondines, mermen – guiding our vessel
    with such precision

onto the rocks – those free-
    marketeers, cutters of corners
at whose hands too it was

a shorter night
    than it might have been
        on Astrolabe Reef.

~

The night before you sailed I dreamt
    the far end of an island flickering
        like a television

    on the blink, around which went
a school of fish-like men
singing as they swam:

        'Roxanne', 'Gloria', 'Amelia' . . .
            random
        women's names. Only then

I realised
    these were neither
        women's names

    nor were they
songs; they were
the names of ships

        at sea. Next thing
            waves were dissolving
        the names, and the ships

were breaking into
smaller, rectangular versions
    of themselves –

red, white, yellow – and
these I recognised as cargo
from the Rena

released
into an oil-black
ocean.

~

It was the last day of spring but
who was counting; it would be
the summer of equations

47,000 tonnes of
the container ship Rena
350 tonnes of bunk oil

in the ocean; 420,000 litres
of crude upended on
the deregulated undersea;

300 oiled birds revived
or not, each day in
the charitable seaside tents

of Papamoa; 2008 blackened
penguins, shearwaters, petrels
scraped off the Bay of Plenty

foreshore. But who wants to know?
A Whakatane fisherman finds
a juvenile minke whale

caked in oil, floating near
White Island, but says nothing. In this
summer of statistics, only

the wash-ins are recorded;
    the ocean is left to dispose
        as it does

    of the rest. Among local fishers
no one dared mention
a dead whale – who could afford

    to have the East Cape
        fisheries
    shut down? Not even

with the Rena
coming apart
    at the seams and

        the seabed covered
    in millions of
glass beads from yet another

broken container – a glimmering
    carpet rolling north,
        then changing direction

    as tide or current dictates. And
hovering nearer the surface
a score of deer pelts

    export-stamped, transfixed
        like kites or else
    breast-stroking shorewards

the waves
stained white from
    a thousand busted sacks

of milk powder. How many barrels
of toxic or
radioactive material now lay

off Astrolabe Reef was anybody's guess
because no one knew
in the first place, where they had been stowed.

Neither the quartermaster
nor the nightwatchmen
on the darkened bridge, those blind men

overseeing nothing – we took this
on board, the two
of us, we counted and surveyed

the depleted fish population,
the 10,000 mislaid shipping containers
reportedly sailing the world's oceans

at any one time, the 4500 kilos of plastic
unknowingly fed to albatross chicks
each year by their parents

and the eighteen vessels which
each day, on average
'explode, sink, collide

capsize or are run aground
abandoned
or set ablaze'.

In these darkest, deregulated days,
you and I came
at last to the 11,000

orange trees of Raoul Island
or what remains
   of them; last season's tally

     126 whales of a morning, breaching
  and travelling, and the woman
we met at the Bowen

earlier today, who recalled, from her time
   on the island, mid-1990s, a Russian-flagged ship
     among the first Kermadec charters.

  Of the paying voyagers, she remembered
an elderly man who
while stationed on Raoul

   a half century earlier, had often swum
     with one particular groper –
a mature fish, he had told her

larger than a grown man.
First night back
   on the island, he fell

    into an argument
  whether or not fish
were sentient beings, his island hosts

adamant, to a man, that
   fish had no memory. Unlike whales.
     In the face of this, gesturing towards

    wetsuit and oxygen tank,
the purpose of his voyage, he said,
was to be reunited

with the giant groper
    remembered from
50 years earlier.

~

Clumps of oil like
    fruit fallen
        from a black tree

all manner of debris
washed as far north
as Coromandel: a Mustang car,

    contents of a family home
        an extensive range of
    Astrolabe wines. As I write this, Felix,

my desk is cluttered with
wooden slats, remnants
    of the Rena we collected from Waihi Beach,

    a cardboard sign in
a child's hand:
'Help Us Save Our Beach

From Ashlee.' It was here
    last January we watched
        graders shunting shipping containers

    along the foreshore, presided over
by security guards
in cowboy hats, while surfers rode in

    on milk-white waves, oblivious
        to the No Swimming signs
    and the sharks which,

attracted by the cargo
of rotting beef, had moved in numbers
        in shore. It was another kind

        of whiteness you spoke of,
    half way up the Kermadec Trench,
steaming north on

HMNZS Canterbury, your vessel
    redirected to investigate
        an unidentified, floating mass.

    Midnight, what appeared, from the bridge
to be an ice-continent
was later confirmed 'a pumice raft'

    the size of a small African nation.
        As the Canterbury
    ploughed its way

through this translucent island
you dreamt onwards
    accompanied by the clunk, rattle

        and squeak of a billion pressurised, aerated
    rocks (eventually traced
to an undersea volcano

just south of L'Esperance, an
    eruption two weeks earlier).
        Sleeping your pumice-enriched sleep

    in a windowless room, while
the ship's hull was being
tended, polished, seen to, in your dreams

you were walking directly beneath
     the pumice raft, striding
across the ocean floor and gazing up

at this long white mineral-cloud
just as, on another morning
     further south, you might have looked up

          from your sea bed and beheld a milk-whiteness
     leaching from the broken containers
of the broken ship Rena.

~

It moves me, the immobility
     of the young, you and
your friends on the aft deck –

Lily, Asia, Susanna
     Tre – your feet dangling
nonchalantly above

undersea citadels, cathedrals
     coral spires – it
moves me, your capacity

to go places yet remain
     so utterly where
you are. Albatross-like

you glide from one thing
     to another, as a great bird
traverses the Kermadec waters

dependent on a
     steady breeze, without so much
as moving

a muscle. In failing wind, however,
    these same birds loll around
mid-ocean for days, waiting

for a breeze to set them
    running, web-footed
across the waters' surface

to regain the air. It is out here
    you are offered a crash course
in the rising and falling world

with your fellow baskers and bathers,
    pedestrians of a running sea
surveyors of this bird-weary ocean –

it is you who are pursued
    by these numbered whales
rectangular

islands and diving birds
    just as the old man
washed back up on Raoul

was pursued
    by the memory of a fish, and
on account of which

his hosts took him each day
    to a carefully calibrated
point offshore, directly

out from Fishing Rock. And
    while the locals
dived or sang

their loud songs, he hovered beneath the boat
    treading water and
waiting, each day yielding a host

of lesser species, uninterested
    shark-life, any number
of Demoiselles, Moorish Idols

not to mention urchins, anemones
    zooplankton and gastropod
but no sign of the groper. On his final day, however

tank-time almost up, the old man
    in the company of three other divers
was about to resurface when

slowly, as if
    from nowhere,
a dark shape

came towards him.
    What might have been
a shadow or oil-slick

was, in fact, an ancient fish
    encrusted in barnacles, weed and
an indefinable sediment.

~

It was a wave
    that delivered us
        to this rock and a rock

    that placed us, shaken
but unbroken,
back upon that wave.

At Fishing Rock, everything inclines
   seawards, the horizon's
shifting population of knotters

and basket-cases, all-night
dance parties on the bridge
   of the Rena, and those politicians

     who would mine the clouds
   for minerals, who would
fish dry land if they could

or sell the sea back
   to itself. We need to remember, Felix,
     we're all cast-offs, blow-ins

     especially here on Raoul Island, with its
crater lakes and
north-facing lawn upon which

     a tui is still trying to dislodge
       the grapefruit from
   its head.

And next morning
once again
   you are all hands

     back on the wide, awakening
   sea, on the aft deck
your tuneful fingers

resuming the melodica. With your
   appropriately entangled lines
     you play

the keyboard at the centre
of the ocean, in the depths of which
the goblin prawn tends

its undersea volcanoes and
a swordfish smokes a
mineral-enriched pipe.

In such company, I arrange
a rendezvous directly above
the Kermadec Trench, between the southward

migrating whales and the northward containers
of the Rena, as observed from
the Rope Room of the Otago

where all these things are tied
together. This way the poem
ends, Felix, is rowed out beyond

Raoul Island, where an old man
in a diving suit hovers amidst the green
constellations of a green undersea

and towards whom a silhouetted form glides
closer and closer,
its fins barely moving, its nose
now pressing softly into

his chest – a gesture of unspeakable
familiarity – dog-like
the groper nuzzles him. With the back of his hand

he strokes the fish's head, at which
the other divers
simultaneously turn away

to resurface as discreetly
    as they can
        as if not to ruffle anything.

    And when, ten minutes later, the old man
finally ascends the rope ladder
airless, spent, he tumbles

    onto the floor of the inflatable and
        lying on his back
    stares upwards at these, the hardy men

of Raoul Island, with their tattoos
and beards, their
    isolation and disbelief, all of them lumped

    speechless in the boat
    wetsuits peeled back, their eyes
red, faces and necks wet with tears.

August 2012 – March 2013
Raoul Island – Waihi Beach – Santiago, Chile

Acknowledgements

Some of these poems first appeared in *PN Review*, *Warwick Review*, *Manchester Review*, *Ika*, *Landfall*, *Art News*, *Griffith Review*, *New Zealand Journal of Interdisciplinary Studies*, *Dominion Post*, *Tui Motu*, *Kermadec: Nine Artists in the South Pacific*, *Kermadec: Art across the Pacific*, Steven Gentry's *Raoul and the Kermadecs* (Steele Roberts, 2013) and Alec Finlay's *Mesostic Herbarium* (Morning Star Editions, Scotland, 2005). Some poems from the first section of this book were included in the limited edition chapbook *Star of Bengal Bank* (animated figure/fernbank studio 2011). 'Whale years' and extracts from 'A book of numbered days' were read at the Museo de Arte Contemporáneo in Santiago de Chile on 17 May 2013, with accompanying Spanish translations by Carolina Miranda and Paula La Monica (these were read by Chilean poet Roberto Onell). Accompanied in Santiago by a live performance on wind instruments by Phil Dadson, 'Whale years' was reprised at Futuna Chapel, Wellington, on 23 March 2014, with Enrique Siqués and Rob Thorne also performing. Poems from the sequence were also set to music by Helen Bowater and are scheduled for performance by the Barefoot Musicians of Budapest, Hungary. 'The return of Christ to Futuna Chapel' was occasioned by the recovery and reinstallation (in March 2013) of the life-sized wooden Christ-figure which had been stolen from the chapel twelve years earlier.

The long poem 'Memory of a fish' was read as part of the annual Turnbull Library Founder's Lecture, June 2013. 'Whale survey, Raoul Island, with Rosemary Dobson' was written upon hearing of the death of the Australian poet and environmentalist in late June 2012. Rosemary and I had corresponded some years earlier and, in the poem, I imagined the ideal time and place for a final conversation. The poem (and Rosemary's 'Poems of the River Wang', upon which it is based) later formed the basis for an installation at the public art space SLOT, Redfern, Sydney, in November 2012. 'The captain of the Rena on Astrolabe Reef' was read at the opening of my exhibition *Whale Years* at Tauranga Art Gallery, October 2014.

Special thanks to all mentioned above and to my other dear friends and fellow Pacific-travellers: Robin Kearns, John Pule, Leilani Tamu, Robin White, Mike Fudakowski, Ruha Fifita, Jason O'Hara, John

Reynolds, Elizabeth Thomson, Warwick Hadwen, Bronwen Golder, George Fyfe, Reuben Friend, Chris Cane, Ernesto Escobar, Amelia Connell, Fiona Hall, Bruce Foster, Euan Macleod and Noel McKenna. I also acknowledge the support of The Pew Charitable Trusts; School of Environment, The University of Auckland; the Royal New Zealand Navy; the Department of Conservation; Luit Bieringa and the National Whale Centre; Nick Bevin and the Futuna Trust; Penny Jackson and the staff of Tauranga Art Gallery; Jenny Neligan and Penney Moir at Bowen Galleries; and Jane Sanders. I am grateful to cover designer Spence Levine and the impeccable Auckland University Press crew: Anna Hodge, Katrina Duncan, Sam Elworthy, Margaret Samuels, Marian Hector and Louisa Kasza; and, of course, special thanks to my family, Jen, Jack-Marcel, Felix and Carlo.

Gregory O'Brien